Penny Wh & Other P

Collected by David Orme

Contents

Penny Whistle Pete 2
My Front Tooth 4
Neversaurus 6
Thirteen Questions 8
Mice Cream 10
I Wasn't Expecting Thursday 12
The Camel's Hump 14
Watch The Puddles 16
Messy Melinda 18
My Hypochondriac Kitchen 20
Tell Me It Isn't! 22
My Grandad 25
The Boy Who Boasted 27

FOLVILLE JUNIOR SCHOOL

Collins Educational
An Imprint of HarperCollinsPublishers

Penny Whistle Pete

Penny Whistle Pete
Was dancing down the street
With a bunch of blue bananas
Tied to both his feet.

He whistled in the morning,
He whistled in the rain,
He whistled while the passengers
Were running for the train.

He never could stop whistling
Even when he needed sleep –
He whistled endless lullabies
Instead of counting sheep.

So if you sense a far off sound
Like a dismal sausage sizzle,
Chances are that what you've heard...
Is Pete's old penny whistle.

Dave Ward

My Front Tooth

When my front tooth came out,
Miss wrapped it in tissue paper
and looked after it for me
until home-time.

When I got home,
I took it out and put it down
on the carpet to examine it.
Just then Samson, our dog,
came bounding in.
Before I could stop him,
he'd gobbled up the tooth
and swallowed it.

"Serves you right
for not looking after it properly,"
said my sister.
"Now you won't get anything
from the tooth fairy."
"I will, won't I, Mum?" I said.
But all she said was,
"Wait and see."

That night,
I put a note under my pillow
explaining what had happened.

In the morning, it had gone.
But there was no sign
of any money.

Feeling fed up, I went downstairs
to let Samson out.
Propped against his basket
was an envelope addressed to
"The Owner of the Lost Tooth".

I tore it open.
Inside there was a note
from The Tooth Fairy,
which said:

"Although your tooth
cannot be found,
the dog's to blame,
so here's your pound".

John Foster

Neversaurus

When dinosaurs roamed the earth,
So huge, it was easy to spot 'em,

You'd frequently see a triceratops,

But never a tricerabottom.

Celia Warren

Thirteen Questions You Should Be Prepared To Answer If You Lose Your Ears At School

Are they clearly named?

When did you notice they were missing?

Were they fixed on properly?

What colour are they?

What size?

Have you looked in the playground?

Did you take them off for P.E.?

Could somebody else have picked them up by mistake?

Have you felt behind
the radiators?

Did you lend them to anybody?

Have you searched the
bottom of your bag?

Does the person you sit next
to have a similar pair?

Are you *sure* you brought
them to school this morning?

John Coldwell

Mice Cream

I know you like ice cream,
But have you tried mice cream?
You eat it with squeaks
And with nibbles.

Please eat it with care,
With your nose in the air,
For it drips and it leaks
And it dribbles.

So comb back your whiskers
And tuck in your tail,
(For the cheese has gone mouldy,
The bread is all stale).

Place paws on a plate
Of this dribblesome dream,
And munch up a mouseful
Of mushy mice cream.

Tony Mitton

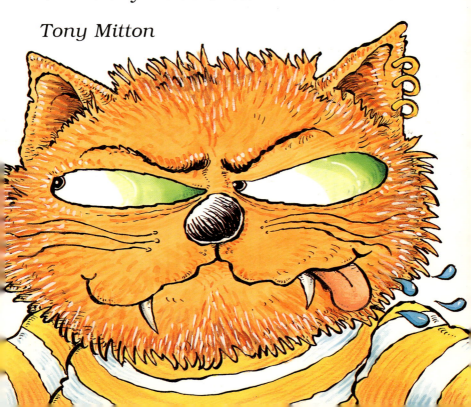

I Wasn't Expecting Thursday

I woke up.
There, at the end of my bed,
looking as mean as
a broken shoelace,
a missed bus,
a forgotten lunch box
and a cut knee,
was

THURSDAY.

It folded its great hairy arms
and barred the way.
"If you ever want to see
Friday again," it growled,
"You'll have to get
past me first."

That's Thursday for you.

John Coldwell

The Camel's Hump

What's in the hump's a mystery
Unparalleled in history.
Some say its there for food and so on –
What evidence have they to go on?
I think it's like an empty tin
For keeping bits and pieces in.

The proof for this is quite immense
If we apply some common sense.
So first let's answer this enquiry –
Where does a camel keep his diary?
Not in a drawer, or on a rack
But tucked up safely on his back.

Where does he store away utensils?
Where does he put his pen and pencils?
Where does he keep his watch all night?
They're hidden safely out of sight,
Not in a bag or plastic sack,
But in the bump upon his back.

And how does a camel
Keep up his hump?
He blows it up
With a bicycle pump!

Charles Thomson

Watch The Puddles

"Watch the puddles,"
said Mum.

I did,
I watched them all day long.
But the puddles didn't
do anything.
They didn't sing,
they didn't dance,
they didn't run...
they weren't much fun.

Just splashed themselves
all over me,
'till I was soaked
from head to toe.

"Now look what you've done,"
said Mum.

Dave Ward

Messy Melinda

Melinda was a scruffy child.
She used to drive her mother wild.
She drove her father to despair,
And changed the colour of his hair.

Her socks, her shoes, her coat, her skirt
Would act like magnets for the dirt.
Her dress, so white to start the day,
By lunch time would be dirty grey.

She always looked an awful mess,
And spilt her dinner down her dress:
Cauliflower, ham and mustard,
Gooseberry pie and lumpy custard.

Messy Melinda didn't care,
And rubbed potato in her hair.
But then she reached the age of three,
And was as sweet as you and me.

Ian Larmont

My Hypochondriac Kitchen

The freezer complains of chilblains, and the whole kitchen starts feeling sorry for itself.

The carpet is depressed, "It's like I'm getting under everyone's feet."

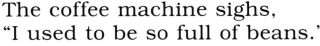

"I feel washed out," says the dishcloth.

"I'm put upon all the time," adds the shelf.

"I can't take the strain anymore," sobs the colander.

The coffee machine sighs, "I used to be so full of beans."

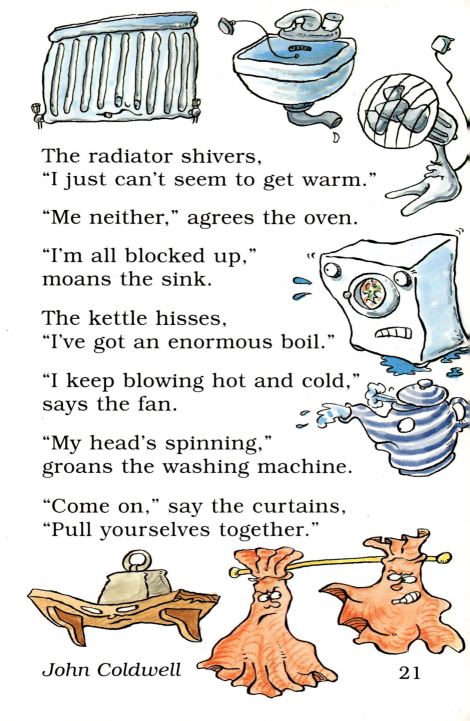

The radiator shivers,
"I just can't seem to get warm."

"Me neither," agrees the oven.

"I'm all blocked up,"
moans the sink.

The kettle hisses,
"I've got an enormous boil."

"I keep blowing hot and cold,"
says the fan.

"My head's spinning,"
groans the washing machine.

"Come on," say the curtains,
"Pull yourselves together."

John Coldwell

Tell Me It Isn't!

Try not to stare
But tell me – what's there?
There isn't a bear
With its head in the air,
Come out of its lair
At the top of the stair,
Is there?

Take care how you speak,
But tell me, that creak,
It isn't the creak of the freak,
The flying freak
With the crooked beak,
About to sneak
Up from behind,
Is it?

Tell me, that sound
Isn't the sound of the hound,
The red-eyed hound
Creeping around,
Dribbling and crunching
The bones it found,
About to leap with one bound
On my back!
It isn't is it?

Tell me, that movement I saw
Behind the door,
It wasn't a paw,
Wasn't a claw,
It wasn't the Beast
About to roar
And pounce and gnaw,
Was it?

I know you told me before,
But I'm still not sure,
So tell me *once* more.

Trevor Millum

My Grandad

My Grandad
is a maniac.

He uses
the wrong side
of the road.

He parks
where he shouldn't.

He never signals...

I sometimes think
he shouldn't be allowed out
on that skateboard.

Bernard Young

The Boy Who Boasted

John Bragger was born
With a very big head.
It grew bigger and bigger
With all that he said.

He boasted, "I'm braver
and better than you."
He boasted so much
That his face became blue,

And he almost arrived
At a premature death
From boasting so much
That he ran out of breath.

"I'm the fastest," he boasted,
"At running in school,"
But everyone knew
That he wasn't at all.

"I'm the quickest at sums,"
He continued, "I'm bright."
(He was quickest but none
Of his answers were right.)

"I'm loudest at singing."
(We won't deny that,
But he sang even worse
Than the caretaker's cat.)

At most things in school, in fact,
John was the worst,
But his head grew so big
That we thought it would burst.

He could only just manage
To squeeze through the door.
We were sure that it couldn't
Increase any more.

But it did
And we even began to feel sorry
When he had to be taken
To school in a lorry.

He carried on boasting
About his success:
"I'm the best playing football.
I'm brilliant at chess."

"I'm dead good at music.
I've made an LP.
They've said I can have
My own show on TV."

"I'm so rich that I'll soon
Be a millionaire."
At times passers-by
Used to gather and stare,

For he couldn't fit now
Into classrooms at all,
And a crane had to lower
Him into the hall.

His brain was no bigger,
I'd say, than a prune,
But his head was the size
Of a hot air balloon.

We thought it might happen,
And it did so one day –
He boasted so much
That he floated away.

He got smaller and smaller
And higher and higher,
Still boasting away
(What a terrible liar):

"My computer's the biggest
That anyone's seen.
Did I tell you last week
I had tea with the Queen?"

"Once I rowed in a boat
Down the Niagara Falls.
My dad is a film star.
My mum's won the pools."

"The American president
Told me next June
I can go in a rocket
And visit the moon."

With hardly a pause
He continued to boast
As he soared over London
And then to the coast.

But where he is now
It seems nobody knows –
I suppose it depends
On the way the wind blows.

(So maybe one day,
If you look up you'll spy
A huge head with legs drifting
High in the sky.)

Our teacher pronounced,
"It's a bit of a mess,"
And various stories
Appeared in the press.

Then the council came round
And collected their crane
And the school returned, almost,
To normal again.

For now that he's gone
I can honestly say
That we miss him a lot
In an odd sort of way.

Charles Thomson